AF688020

The Solopreneur's Survival Kit

Essential Tools and Techniques for Managing Finances, Marketing, and Customer Relations

Lysander Winchester

Table of Contents

1 Financial Foundations

Understanding your financial landscape is paramount for solopreneur success. Ignoring this crucial element can lead to unforeseen challenges, jeopardizing your entire venture. Think of it like building a house—you wouldn't start constructing walls without a solid foundation, would you? Similarly, a strong financial foundation is non-negotiable for a thriving solo business. This means actively managing your income, diligently tracking your expenses, and consistently monitoring your cash flow. Procrastination in this area could lead to significant setbacks and eventually failure. Building a robust financial plan from the beginning will greatly reduce the risk of these serious problems. This should involve forecasting income, budgeting realistically, and having an emergency fund in place. This proactive approach helps to manage the uncertainty inherent in running a new business.

Creating a realistic budget isn't about deprivation; it's about informed decision-making. It's about strategically allocating your resources to maximize your potential for growth and profitability. Start by identifying all your income sources, including both projected and current. Then, meticulously list all your expenses, both business-related and personal. You'd be surprised how easily smaller expenses can add up over time. Categorize these expenses (rent, utilities, marketing, materials, etc.) for easier analysis and to quickly identify potential areas for cost reduction. Remember to include a cushion for unexpected costs – emergencies happen, and preparation is key. Your budget should be a living document, reviewed and adjusted regularly as your business evolves.

Effective expense tracking is more than just noting what you spent; it's about understanding why you spent it and whether that expenditure aligns with your business goals. Use accounting software or a simple spreadsheet to meticulously record every transaction. This detailed record will illuminate spending patterns, highlighting areas where you might be overspending. This approach is crucial for tax purposes and helps you make informed decisions about future spending. For instance, if you find a significant portion of your budget is going towards advertising that isn't generating leads, you can adjust your strategy. By clearly seeing where your money is going, you can optimize your spending and improve your profitability. Don't underestimate the power of this simple yet effective technique; it's the backbone of sound financial management.

Regularly reviewing your financial statements is critical to staying on top of your financial health. This means analyzing your income and expenses, comparing them to your budget, and identifying any discrepancies. Are you consistently exceeding or falling short of your projected income? Are your expenses higher than anticipated? Understanding these trends will allow you to adjust your strategies accordingly. This consistent monitoring provides an early warning system for potential problems. If you discover a negative trend, you can implement corrective measures before the problem becomes insurmountable. Ignoring these warning signs can lead to serious financial trouble. By being proactive and regularly evaluating your financial performance, you ensure a stable and sustainable business.

Building an emergency fund is not just a good idea; it's a necessity. Unexpected expenses, like equipment malfunctions or a sudden drop in sales, can easily derail your business if you're not prepared. Aim to save enough to cover at least three to six months of your operating expenses. This safety net will provide peace of mind and prevent you from having to make drastic decisions during difficult times. Think of it as insurance for your business, protecting it from unexpected financial storms. This financial buffer will allow you to navigate difficult periods without sacrificing your business's long-term health. Remember, financial stability isn't just about making money; it's also about safeguarding what you've earned. A substantial emergency fund ensures your survival during unpredictable situations.

Understanding basic accounting principles is also vital. You don't need to become a CPA, but grasping fundamental concepts like income statements, balance sheets, and cash flow statements is essential. These statements provide a clear picture of your business's financial health. They help you understand profitability, liquidity, and overall financial performance. Numerous resources are available, including online courses and books, to help you learn these concepts at your own pace. The time spent acquiring this foundational knowledge will pay off immensely in the long run. Knowing how to interpret these statements allows you to make informed decisions based on concrete data, rather than relying on guesswork.

Finally, seek professional advice when needed. While you can handle many aspects of your finances yourself, consider consulting a financial advisor or accountant, especially when making significant decisions. A professional can offer objective guidance and support, helping you avoid costly mistakes. They can provide expert insights into tax strategies, financial planning, and other crucial financial matters. Their experience and expertise can be invaluable, particularly in the initial stages of your business. Don't hesitate to seek expert help; it's an investment in your business's future success. The cost of professional guidance is far outweighed by the potential benefits of avoiding costly errors.

1.1 Budgeting Basics

Creating a budget as a solopreneur isn't about strict limitations; it's about informed choices. Think of it as a roadmap guiding your financial journey, ensuring you reach your business goals without running out of fuel. It's a dynamic tool, not a rigid structure; adapt it as your business evolves and learns.

Start by honestly assessing your current financial situation. List all your income streams, be it freelance projects, recurring subscriptions, or any other revenue source. Don't underestimate the importance of accuracy here; a clear picture of your income is fundamental to effective budgeting. Then, categorize your income to understand where your money's coming from and how each stream contributes to your overall revenue. This will aid in future financial forecasting and strategy development.

Next, meticulously track your expenses. This involves noting every single outflow of funds. Don't gloss over small purchases; those seemingly insignificant amounts accumulate quickly. Use budgeting apps or spreadsheets, whatever works best for you. Categorize these expenses—office supplies, marketing costs, software subscriptions, etc. This organized view reveals areas where you might be overspending. Tracking expenses doesn't just reveal overspending; it helps understand spending habits, pinpoint crucial business investments, and even aids in finding tax deductions.

Now, let's align your income and expenses. Subtract your total expenses from your total income. This reveals your profit or loss. A negative figure isn't necessarily a disaster; it highlights areas needing attention. You might need to increase revenue, cut expenses, or perhaps reassess your pricing strategy. A positive number signifies progress, but it's essential to continue monitoring and analyzing to maintain financial stability. Understanding your profit and loss isn't merely about numbers; it's a vital insight into the health of your business, helping you make sound decisions to achieve business sustainability.

Allocate your budget strategically. Decide how much you need to allocate towards essential business expenses, like software, marketing, and supplies. Then, allocate funds for your personal living expenses. Remember, you're a business owner and an individual who needs to be supported. Set aside money for taxes, as well. Ignoring this can lead to significant financial penalties down the line; it's not just about compliance; it's about long-term financial health for your business.

Regularly review and adjust your budget. Your business won't stay stagnant; it will grow and change. Your budget must reflect this growth and any shifts in your revenue or expenses. Review it monthly, or even weekly if needed. Flexibility and adaptation are crucial; budgets should be your guide, not your constraint. Consistent review is not just about numbers; it helps anticipate changes and adjust strategies based on evolving realities.

Don't be afraid to seek help. If you're struggling to create or manage your budget, there are resources available. Consult with a financial advisor or accountant. They can provide personalized advice and guidance suited to your specific circumstances. External help is not about admitting failure; it's an intelligent approach toward professional business development.

Remember, budgeting isn't a one-time task; it's an ongoing process. It's about taking control of your finances, making informed decisions, and setting your business up for long-term success. Approach it as a continuous journey of learning and adaptation, not a rigid set of rules to follow. It's a foundational step toward sustainable business practices and a fulfilling entrepreneurial path. The key takeaway is this: a well-managed budget ensures your solopreneur venture thrives, not just survives. It provides stability, guiding your decisions, ensuring you remain in charge of your financial destiny. Your budget is your financial compass, guiding you toward your business goals and supporting sustainable long-term growth.

1.2 Tracking Expenses

Accurate expense tracking is the bedrock of financial health for any solopreneur. Without it, you're essentially navigating in the dark, making decisions based on gut feeling rather than hard data. This lack of clarity can lead to missed opportunities, financial instability, and ultimately, the failure of your business. Therefore, establishing a robust expense tracking system from day one is non-negotiable.

Begin by choosing a method that suits your personality and technological comfort level. Some prefer pen and paper, finding the tactile experience aids their memory and focus. Others might embrace sophisticated accounting software, utilizing features like automated categorization and reporting. No matter your choice, consistency is paramount. Irregular or incomplete tracking renders the entire exercise futile.

Regardless of your chosen method, categorization is crucial. Instead of simply listing expenses, group them into meaningful categories like office supplies, marketing, travel, and client entertainment. This level of detail allows you to identify spending patterns and potential areas for savings. For example, perhaps you're spending far more on marketing materials than anticipated, requiring a reevaluation of your marketing strategy. Or maybe you notice a high proportion of your income is tied up in travel, prompting a review of your methods of client communication.

Don't underestimate the power of receipts. While digital transactions automatically record many expenses, always retain physical receipts for purchases. They are your proof of expenditure and vital in case of audits or tax investigations. Develop a system for organizing them, perhaps using a labeled folder or filing system, to ensure you can easily retrieve them when needed. Keep your receipts safe. Their loss could present serious problems.

Consider utilizing expense tracking apps. Many excellent applications are available, both free and paid, that simplify the entire process. Some integrate with your bank accounts, automatically categorizing transactions and generating reports. Others offer features such as mileage tracking and invoice generation, which are especially valuable for entrepreneurs who travel frequently for business or bill clients for their services. Explore these to see how they can improve your financial overview.

Regular review is essential. Don't just track your expenses; actively analyze them. Schedule time each week or month to examine your spending patterns. Look for anomalies, unexpected spikes in certain categories, and areas where you might cut back. This proactive approach enables you to make informed decisions and adjust your budget accordingly. Ignoring this critical step leaves you vulnerable to financial surprises. You should know where your money is going.

Remember, expense tracking isn't a mere bookkeeping exercise; it's a strategic tool. The data you collect provides crucial insights into your business's financial health. It helps you identify profitable areas, highlight inefficiencies, and make data-driven decisions that can positively impact your business's bottom line. This insight will enable you to take more intelligent action, making your decisions more purposeful and effective. Remember to stay on top of your expenses.

By meticulously tracking your expenses, you gain a clear understanding of your cash flow, allowing for more accurate budgeting and financial forecasting. This information empowers you to make well-informed decisions, reducing financial stress and promoting the long-term sustainability of your business. This is crucial for your success. Remember that this meticulous process is a major investment in your business's future. Don't treat it as a chore; view it as a key component of your business strategy.

The benefits extend beyond simple cost savings. Accurate expense records are also crucial for tax purposes. At the end of the financial year, you'll need to compile these records to file your taxes accurately and efficiently. Proper documentation protects you from potential penalties or audits, further emphasizing the importance of consistent and accurate expense tracking. This aspect alone is worth the effort involved.

Finally, remember that expense tracking is an ongoing process. It's not a one-time activity; it requires consistent effort and commitment. But the rewards far outweigh the effort. By building this strong foundation of financial awareness, you significantly increase your chances of solopreneur success. This diligence and attention to detail will pay off significantly. Make it a habit.

2 Smart Marketing Strategies

Defining your ideal customer is paramount. Understanding their needs, pain points, and aspirations allows you to tailor your marketing message for maximum impact. This isn't about generic appeals; it's about speaking directly to the specific individuals most likely to become paying clients. Research your market thoroughly. Use online tools, surveys, and competitor analysis to build a comprehensive profile. What are their demographics? What platforms do they frequent? What kind of content resonates with them? The more you know, the more effectively you can target your efforts. Remember, precision marketing trumps blanket advertising every time.

Creating a strong online presence is more than just having a website; it's about building a brand that inspires trust and credibility. Your website should be professional, easy to navigate, and visually appealing, reflecting the quality of your services. Ensure your contact information is readily available and that your website is optimized for search engines. Use relevant keywords and high-quality images to improve your search engine rankings (SEO). Think about your brand story – what makes you unique and why should people choose you? Craft a compelling narrative that resonates with your target audience and differentiates you from the competition.

Social media offers unparalleled opportunities for connecting with potential clients. However, it's crucial to choose the right platforms for your target audience. Don't spread yourself too thin trying to manage every platform. Instead, focus your efforts on the networks where your ideal customers are most active. Consistency is key – regular posting keeps you top-of-mind with your audience. Engage with your followers, respond to comments and messages promptly, and participate in relevant conversations. Remember that social media is a two-way street; it's about building relationships, not just broadcasting your message. Authenticity is vital; people can spot insincerity a mile away.

Content marketing is about providing valuable information to your audience, establishing yourself as an expert in your field. Create high-quality content that addresses their needs and provides solutions to their problems. This could be anything from blog posts and articles to videos, infographics, and podcasts. Consider the different content formats and determine which ones are most effective for your audience. High-quality, engaging content not only attracts potential clients but also builds brand loyalty and fosters trust. Think of your content as a means of educating and entertaining your audience, subtly highlighting your expertise along the way.

Email marketing remains a highly effective tool for nurturing leads and building relationships with clients. Build an email list by offering valuable incentives, such as free ebooks or webinars, in exchange for email addresses. Segment your list to target specific audience groups with tailored messages. Avoid generic blasts and focus on personalized communication that adds value to the recipient's inbox. Consistent email marketing can cultivate strong relationships and keeps you top of mind with your audience. Remember, it's about building connections, not just selling products or services. Use email to share valuable information, answer their questions, and establish yourself as a trusted advisor.

Paid advertising can be a powerful tool for reaching a wider audience, particularly when combined with organic marketing strategies. Platforms like Google Ads and social media ads offer targeted advertising options, allowing you to reach specific demographics and interests. However, it's crucial to track your results closely and adjust your campaigns accordingly. Don't waste money on ineffective ads; analyze your data to identify what's working and what's not. Always set a budget and stick to it. Remember that paid advertising is just one piece of the puzzle; it should be used in conjunction with other marketing tactics to achieve maximum impact.

Analyzing your results and making data-driven decisions are essential for optimizing your marketing efforts. Use analytics tools to track your website traffic, social media engagement, and email open rates. Identify what's working well and what needs improvement. Don't be afraid to experiment with different strategies and adapt your approach based on the data you collect. Regularly review your marketing plan, making adjustments as needed to ensure you're consistently reaching your target audience and achieving your goals. Marketing is an ongoing process; it requires constant monitoring, analysis, and adaptation to stay ahead of the curve. Continuous improvement is crucial for long-term success.

2.1 Online Presence

Your online presence is the digital storefront of your business. It's the first impression many potential clients will have, so making it professional, engaging, and informative is paramount. A strong online presence isn't just about having a website; it's about strategically using various online platforms to reach your target audience and build credibility. Think of it like this: if someone searches for your services online, you want them to find you easily. This requires more than just a website. You need to optimize your website and other online properties for search engines. This process, known as Search Engine Optimization (SEO), is crucial for attracting organic traffic—customers finding you without paid advertising. Keyword research plays a vital role. By identifying the terms your ideal clients use when searching for services like yours, you can tailor your online content to match. This increases the likelihood of your website appearing high in search engine results. Beyond that, you need a compelling website design. It should be clean, easy to navigate, and mobile-friendly, ensuring a positive user experience for visitors on any device. In short, your website needs to effectively communicate your unique value proposition, showcase your expertise, and encourage visitors to take action—whether that's contacting you, booking a consultation, or making a purchase.

Beyond your website, a crucial aspect of your online presence involves leveraging social media platforms. Each platform has a unique audience and requires a tailored approach. For example, LinkedIn is ideal for connecting with professionals and building B2B relationships. Meanwhile, platforms like Instagram or Pinterest could be more effective for visually driven businesses showcasing their work or products. Consistency is key; regularly posting high-quality, relevant content that engages your audience is vital. This doesn't mean posting incessantly; it's about delivering valuable information and fostering a community around your brand. Interact with comments, respond to messages, and participate in relevant conversations. Remember, social media is a two-way street. Use relevant hashtags to increase visibility and consider using paid advertising on platforms like Facebook or Instagram to reach a wider audience, carefully targeting your ideal customer profile. This helps you reach more people in your niche, increasing potential customers.

Online reviews significantly impact your online presence. Positive reviews build trust and credibility, influencing potential clients' decisions. Encourage satisfied clients to leave reviews on platforms like Google My Business, Yelp, or industry-specific review sites. Responding to both positive and negative reviews demonstrates professionalism and accountability. Addressing negative reviews constructively, showcasing your commitment to customer satisfaction, can turn a negative experience into a positive one. This shows prospective clients that you care about their feedback and are willing to resolve any issues.

Building a strong online presence takes time and effort. It's an ongoing process, not a one-time project. Regularly review and update your online content to ensure it remains relevant and engaging. Stay up-to-date with the latest trends and algorithms to maintain your online visibility. Analyze your website traffic and social media engagement using analytics tools to identify what's working and what needs improvement. This data-driven approach allows for constant refinement and optimization, maximizing your online reach and impact. Consider using a professional email address that reflects your business name; this adds a layer of professionalism that free email addresses often lack. Also, ensure that your online presence across all platforms maintains a consistent brand identity, from logos and color palettes to messaging and tone of voice. This consistency creates a cohesive and recognizable brand, strengthening your overall online identity. This ensures that your brand remains memorable and easily identified by your target audience. Finally, remember that your online presence is an extension of your brand.

It should accurately reflect your values, expertise, and commitment to customer service, building trust and loyalty among your audience.

2.2 Social Media Power

Harnessing the power of social media is crucial for any solopreneur. It's not just about having a presence; it's about strategically using these platforms to connect with your ideal clients, build brand awareness, and ultimately, drive sales. Think of social media as your virtual storefront, open 24/7, reaching a global audience. The key is to understand which platforms are most relevant to your target market and to tailor your content accordingly. Don't spread yourself too thin trying to be everywhere at once; focus your energy on where your ideal clients spend their time online.

Knowing your audience is paramount. Before posting a single update, thoroughly research your ideal client's online habits. What platforms do they frequent? What kind of content resonates with them? What are their pain points, and how can your offerings alleviate those? Understanding these aspects will significantly impact the effectiveness of your social media strategy. Consider creating detailed buyer personas, including demographics, interests, and online behavior. This detailed understanding will guide your content creation and ensure your message reaches the right people.

Content is king, but consistency is queen. Regularly posting high-quality, engaging content is key to building a loyal following. Think about the value you offer your audience; focus on providing helpful information, insightful tips, and entertaining content that aligns with your brand. Remember to maintain a consistent posting schedule to keep your audience engaged and expecting new material. This cultivates anticipation and ensures your content remains top-of-mind for potential clients. Experiment with various content formats—videos, images, infographics, and stories—to keep your feed fresh and interesting. Don't underestimate the power of visual content; a compelling image or video can often speak louder than words.

Engage authentically with your audience. Social media isn't a one-way street. It's about building relationships and fostering a sense of community. Respond to comments and messages promptly, participate in relevant conversations, and ask questions to encourage interaction. Genuine engagement builds trust and loyalty, turning followers into advocates for your business. Don't just broadcast; have real conversations. Consider running polls, hosting Q&A sessions, and responding personally to comments to enhance the interaction. This personalized touch can significantly increase engagement and build stronger relationships with your followers.

Track your results and adjust your strategy accordingly. Social media analytics are invaluable tools for measuring the effectiveness of your efforts. Monitor key metrics like engagement, reach, and website traffic to understand what's working and what's not. Use this data to refine your strategy, experiment with new approaches, and optimize your content for maximum impact. Don't be afraid to experiment; what works for one business might not work for another. Continuous monitoring and adaptation are key to achieving consistent growth on social media. The tools provided by most platforms give you insights into your audience's demographics, engagement patterns, and post performance, enabling you to make data-driven decisions.

Remember, social media is a long-term game. Building a strong online presence and cultivating a loyal following takes time and effort. Don't expect overnight success; be patient, persistent, and consistent in your efforts. Focus on building authentic relationships with your audience, providing valuable content, and engaging consistently. Over time, your efforts will pay off, leading to increased brand awareness, lead generation, and ultimately, business growth. Success comes from thoughtful planning, consistent execution, and a willingness to adapt your strategy as needed. Regularly review your overall strategy, making adjustments based on what you learn.

Consider using social media scheduling tools to maintain consistency even when you are busy. These tools allow you to prepare and schedule posts in advance, ensuring a steady stream of engaging content. This frees up your time to focus on other critical aspects of your business, while maintaining a strong online presence. Proper use of these scheduling tools not only saves you time but ensures optimal scheduling based on audience engagement trends.

Don't neglect the power of paid advertising. While organic reach is important, paid social media ads can significantly accelerate your growth. Targeted advertising allows you to reach specific demographics and interests, ensuring your message is seen by the right people. Start with a small budget and experiment with different ad formats and targeting options to determine what works best for your business. Carefully track your return on investment (ROI) to make sure your advertising budget is used efficiently. Efficient ad management can significantly improve your campaign performance and increase return on investment. Remember to A/B test different ad creatives and targeting options to optimize your ad campaigns.

Finally, remember that social media is only one piece of the puzzle. While it's a powerful tool for reaching potential clients, it's not a standalone solution. Combine your social media efforts with other marketing strategies, such as email marketing, content marketing, and networking, to create a holistic approach that maximizes your reach and impact. A multi-pronged marketing strategy provides a more comprehensive and effective reach, ensuring your business is visible across various channels. Integrating social media with other strategies provides a synergistic effect, amplifying the impact of your marketing efforts.

2.3 Content Creation

Content creation is the lifeblood of your online marketing. It's not just about churning out posts; it's about strategically crafting messages that resonate with your ideal clients, building trust, and ultimately driving conversions. Forget generic content; your goal is to establish yourself as a thought leader within your niche.

Think of your content as a conversation, not a broadcast. Your audience wants to connect with a real person, someone who understands their problems and offers valuable solutions. Inject your personality into your writing. Let your passion and expertise shine through; authenticity is key. Don't be afraid to be yourself. Your unique perspective is what will set you apart. Remember those quirky details that make you, you? Share them; it will help your audience feel like they know, like and trust you.

Developing a consistent content calendar is essential for maintaining momentum and reaching your target audience effectively. Don't just throw together content; a structured approach maximizes your impact. Plan your content well in advance. Consider thematic weeks or monthly focuses to create a cohesive narrative. This doesn't mean rigidly sticking to a schedule; allow for flexibility and adapt as needed. Listen to your audience; respond to what they are seeking from you. That's how you build a loyal following.

Visuals significantly enhance engagement. People are visual creatures; striking images and compelling videos hold their attention far better than walls of text. Use high-quality images that are relevant to your message; poorly chosen imagery can detract from even the most well-written content. Consider investing in professional photography or using royalty-free images from reputable sources. Similarly, if videos are appropriate for your audience and your brand, invest your time in making engaging videos for your business to reach even more people.

Mastering different content formats is crucial for reaching a broader audience and keeping your content fresh. Experiment with blog posts, short-form videos, infographics, podcasts – whatever works best for your audience and your expertise. Don't limit yourself to a single platform or format. Diversify your approach to maximize your reach and ensure you're connecting with people on their terms.

Repurposing your content is a powerful way to increase visibility and efficiency. That excellent blog post you spent hours crafting? Turn it into a series of social media posts, an infographic, or even a short video. You've already put in the work; leverage it to its full potential. Doing so will also allow you to experiment with different marketing strategies in the meanwhile.

Engagement is about more than just posting; it's about fostering a genuine two-way communication. Respond to comments and messages promptly and thoughtfully. Ask questions and encourage interaction. Create a community around your brand. This doesn't mean spending every waking moment glued to your social media; it's about thoughtfully fostering meaningful conversations.

Analyze your results to see what resonates with your audience and what doesn't. What content performs best? Which platforms are driving the most engagement? Use analytics to inform your strategy. Don't just create content and hope for the best; track your results and adjust accordingly. A little work here and there can go a long way in the long run.

Remember your website's role as a central hub for all your content. Optimize your blog posts with relevant keywords for better search engine visibility. Ensure your website is easy to navigate and visually appealing. Your website is your online storefront; it needs to be functional, appealing, and easy to navigate for your audience.

Finally, consistency is key. Don't expect overnight success. Build your audience and establish your authority gradually. Regular, high-quality content consistently over time will bring you the results you seek. This is a marathon, not a sprint. Maintaining a strong and consistent presence requires effort, dedication, and a deep understanding of your audience. This will ultimately lead to increased visibility and growth for your business.

3 Client Acquisition

Developing a robust client acquisition strategy is paramount for any solopreneur's success. It's not simply about attracting anyone; it's about attracting the right clients—those who value your services and are a good fit for your business model. This involves a multifaceted approach, integrating several key techniques.

Effective networking is more than just exchanging business cards. It's about building genuine relationships. Attend industry events, join relevant online communities, and actively participate in conversations. Focus on providing value to others; offer your expertise freely, and listen attentively to their needs. Remember, networking is a two-way street; nurture those connections, and you'll find that referrals and opportunities naturally emerge. Don't just collect contacts, cultivate relationships.

Lead generation is about strategically attracting potential clients. This could involve creating valuable content, such as blog posts, webinars, or e-books, which attract individuals interested in your niche. Optimize your website for search engines, ensuring potential clients can easily find you when searching for services like yours. Consider targeted advertising on social media platforms or through Google Ads, focusing your efforts on reaching the specific demographics that most value your offering. These methods allow you to cultivate a steady flow of leads.

Sales strategies extend beyond closing deals. It's about understanding your ideal client, their pain points, and how your services provide solutions. Develop a clear and concise value proposition that highlights the benefits of working with you. Practice your pitch, refining it until it's both compelling and informative. Master the art of listening to client needs, tailoring your approach to each individual. Successful selling is about genuinely helping clients solve their problems.

Onboarding new clients sets the tone for your working relationship. Develop a clear and structured onboarding process that makes clients feel valued and supported from day one. Provide them with all the necessary information, expectations, and next steps. A smooth onboarding experience not only builds trust but also sets the stage for a successful and long-lasting collaboration, leading to positive reviews and more referrals. This is crucial to making a good first impression and setting realistic expectations.

Pricing your services is critical for profitability and ensuring you're fairly compensated for your expertise. Research your competitors, analyze your costs, and determine a price that reflects your value. Remember to clearly communicate your pricing structure to avoid any confusion or misunderstanding with your clients. Don't undervalue your skills; you deserve to earn a sustainable income. Consider different pricing models, like hourly rates, project-based fees, or subscription services, to find the approach that best suits your business and clients' needs.

Ultimately, client acquisition isn't a one-time event; it's an ongoing process. By combining effective networking, strategic lead generation, compelling sales techniques, a smooth onboarding process, and fair pricing, you create a sustainable system for attracting and retaining high-value clients. Remember, success in this area is not a sprint, but a marathon—consistent effort and refinement are key. Continuously evaluating and adjusting your strategy based on results is vital for long-term growth and prosperity. The key is to remain flexible, adaptable and responsive to client feedback and market changes. This allows you to constantly refine your approach to ensure the most effective and sustainable client acquisition strategy. Regularly review your approach and adapt to the dynamic nature of client needs. The marketplace is constantly evolving, and your strategies must evolve with it.

3.1 Networking Skills

Networking, for the solopreneur, isn't just about collecting business cards; it's about cultivating genuine connections that translate into opportunities. Think of it less as a transactional exchange and more as the planting of seeds that, nurtured properly, will yield a bountiful harvest of clients and collaborations. It requires a strategic approach, a consistent effort, and a genuine interest in others – not just what they can do for you.

The most effective networking happens organically. Don't force it. Attend industry events, workshops, and conferences, but focus on actively listening and engaging in conversations. Ask questions, genuinely show interest in the work others do, and share your own experiences, highlighting your unique value proposition subtly. Avoid sounding like a sales pitch; instead, aim for meaningful exchanges.

Online networking platforms offer a different landscape, but the principles remain the same. Engage thoughtfully in relevant groups and forums, contributing valuable insights and offering help where you can. Don't just self-promote; offer assistance to others, build your reputation as a knowledgeable and helpful professional. Remember, online net-

working is about building trust and relationships just like offline networking. Consider LinkedIn as a vital tool, a place where you can showcase your expertise and actively participate in discussions related to your niche.
Following up is crucial. After meeting someone at an event or connecting online, send a personalized message expressing your appreciation for the conversation. Reiterate a point you found particularly interesting from your discussion. This not only reinforces the connection but also keeps you top of mind. A simple follow-up email or LinkedIn message can make a significant difference in converting a brief encounter into a lasting professional relationship. Think of it as watering the seeds you've planted.
Remember that networking is a marathon, not a sprint. It's a long-term strategy that requires consistent effort and patience. Don't get discouraged if you don't see immediate results. Focus on building genuine relationships and providing value. Over time, your network will grow, and the opportunities will naturally follow.
Consider diversifying your networking strategies. Don't rely solely on industry events. Explore opportunities to network within your local community, join professional organizations, or volunteer your time for causes you care about. These activities can introduce you to people outside your immediate industry, broadening your network and exposing you to unexpected opportunities. Remember that relationships are built on trust, consistency and mutual respect.
Always be mindful of the information you share. Protect your intellectual property and avoid divulging sensitive business information prematurely. Build trust slowly and strategically, knowing that every interaction represents your brand. Your integrity and reliability will eventually be

your most valuable currency.
Networking, in its essence, is about reciprocity. Be prepared to offer assistance and support to others in your network. Help them with their challenges and celebrate their successes. This reciprocal approach fosters strong relationships built on mutual respect and trust and ultimately serves as the foundation of a sustainable and fulfilling career. It's about building a community, not just a list of contacts.
Finally, track your networking efforts. Keep a record of the people you meet, the events you attend, and the follow-up actions you take. This helps you monitor your progress and identify areas for improvement. Regularly review your network and identify opportunities for deeper engagement. It's a continuous journey of cultivation and expansion, not a static list. Treat your network as an asset, something that requires ongoing care and attention. A well-maintained network will yield significant returns for years to come, supporting your growth and success as a solopreneur. Remember the power of personal connections. They can be the foundation of a thriving and sustainable business. The key is to approach networking with a genuine desire to connect, rather than merely seeking transactional benefits. Authenticity and genuine interest in others will always yield the best results.

3.2 Lead Generation

Generating leads, the lifeblood of any solopreneur's business, requires a multifaceted approach. It's not a single tactic, but a strategic blend of methods tailored to your specific niche and target audience. Think of it as building a fishing net, not just casting a single line.
Content marketing forms a critical part of this net. Regularly creating valuable, informative content — blog posts, articles, videos, infograph-

ics — positions you as an expert in your field. This attracts potential clients who are actively searching for solutions you offer. Remember, consistency is key; a sporadic content calendar won't yield consistent results. Think strategically about what problems your potential clients face; address those concerns directly through your content, subtly guiding them towards your services as the solution.

Leveraging social media is equally important. It's not just about posting updates; it's about engaging with your audience, responding to comments, and participating in relevant conversations. Each platform has its own nuances. LinkedIn, for example, leans professional, ideal for B2B interactions. Instagram might be perfect for visually appealing content that speaks to a more general audience. Don't spread yourself too thin; focus your energy on the platforms that best serve your target demographic. Use a consistent brand voice and aesthetic across all platforms for optimal recognition and recall.

Networking, both online and offline, shouldn't be underestimated. Attending industry events, joining relevant online communities, and proactively connecting with potential clients can lead to unexpected opportunities. Remember, genuine connections are more valuable than superficial interactions. Focus on building relationships, offering value to others, and subtly showcasing your expertise without being overly self-promotional. Active participation in industry forums and comment sections can demonstrate your knowledge and build credibility. Don't just consume content—contribute to it.

Email marketing remains a powerful tool. Building an email list allows you to directly communicate with interested individuals, nurturing leads through valuable content and targeted offers. However, respect your subscribers' inboxes; avoid bombarding them with unsolicited messages. Instead, provide them with regular, high-quality content that adds value to their lives. Segment your list based on interests and buying behavior to personalize your messages and increase engagement. Remember that effective email marketing requires careful planning and a clear understanding of your audience's needs.

Paid advertising, such as Google Ads or social media ads, can accelerate lead generation. However, it's crucial to carefully plan your campaigns, targeting the right demographics and using compelling ad copy. Don't just throw money at ads; track your results carefully and adjust your strategy accordingly. Understanding your target audience and their online behavior is paramount to effective ad spending. Experiment with different ad formats and targeting options to optimize your ROI. Remember to track your key performance indicators and analyze your data regularly to refine your strategy.

Finally, optimizing your website for search engines (SEO) is critical. Ensure your website is easy to navigate, loads quickly, and contains relevant keywords that potential clients would search for. Regularly updating your website with fresh content also signals to search engines that your site is active and relevant, thus boosting your rankings in search results. Focus on providing valuable content that satisfies user search intent. Internal linking between pages on your website can further improve SEO, guiding users through your content and potentially converting them into customers. In essence, effective SEO acts as a powerful, organic lead generation engine. Remember, SEO is an ongoing process, not a one-time fix.

3.3 Sales Strategies

Understanding your ideal client is paramount. Before you even think about a sales pitch, delve deep into who you're trying to reach. What are their pain points? What keeps them up at night? What are their aspirations? The more intimately you know your target audience, the more effectively you can tailor your message and your sales approach. This isn't about generic marketing; it's about building a genuine connection based on understanding. Think of it as creating a bespoke solution, not a mass-produced product. This requires research, observation, and a willingness to listen more than you speak, initially. Analyze your current clients—what are their common traits? Where did they find you? What resonated with them most? This intimate knowledge fuels your sales strategy. Learning your ideal client inside and out is your most powerful tool.

Crafting a compelling value proposition is the next critical step. This isn't just about listing features; it's about articulating the tangible benefits your service provides. Think in terms of the transformation you offer, not just the tasks you perform. For instance, instead of saying "I design websites," you might say, "I create websites that attract high-quality leads and boost your sales." This subtly shifts the focus from the activity to the outcome, appealing directly to your client's desires. Make it concise, memorable, and easily understood, even by someone outside your industry. Test different versions, seeing what resonates best with potential clients. It's an iterative process, refinement is essential. Once you've created a compelling value proposition, weave it into all your communication materials.

Sales isn't about pushing a product; it's about building relationships. Develop a genuine interest in your clients' needs and challenges. Listen actively during conversations, asking clarifying questions to ensure you fully understand their situation. This approach establishes trust and rapport, creating a foundation for long-term collaboration. Remember, people buy from people they like and trust. Think of it like a dance; it's a two-way street of communication, understanding, and shared goals. Build that relationship early on to lay the foundation for successful sales conversations and repeat business. Always keep in mind that empathy is your superpower in sales.

Mastering the art of storytelling is incredibly powerful. Weave narratives into your sales presentations, using case studies or anecdotes to illustrate the value of your services. This makes your message more relatable and engaging, making it easier for potential clients to visualize the benefits. Humans are naturally drawn to stories; they provide context, emotion, and credibility. Sharing success stories showcases your capabilities and builds confidence in your abilities. Remember the details—the challenges, the solutions, the results. Paint a vivid picture that helps the potential client see themselves achieving similar successes.

Effective communication is key to sales success. This encompasses both written and verbal communication. Ensure your marketing materials, website copy, and sales pitches are clear, concise, and easy to understand. Avoid jargon and technical terms that might confuse potential clients. Always tailor your communication to your specific audience, understanding their background, expertise, and language. Practice your delivery. Clear and confident communication builds trust, ensuring that the message is received perfectly and leaves the desired impact. Practice explaining your service in multiple ways, adapting to your audience's needs and understanding. Excellent communication skills are your secret weapon.

Don't be afraid to ask for the sale. Many solopreneurs hesitate to explicitly ask for business, fearing rejection. However, a clear and confident call to action is essential. Frame your request in a way that's both professional and persuasive. Offer different packages or options to cater to various budgets and needs. Remember, a "no" today might be a "yes" tomorrow. Persistence is key. Follow up with potential clients after your initial interaction, providing additional information or answering any outstanding questions. This follow-up helps nurture relationships and keep your business top of mind. Don't be afraid to personalize your follow-up messages.

Finally, always follow up and stay organized. After a sales call or meeting, send a thank-you note summarizing the key points of the conversation and outlining the next steps. Use a CRM system to track your interactions with potential clients, ensuring you don't miss any opportunities. Remember that building a successful business takes time and consistent effort. Be patient, persistent, and always strive to improve your sales techniques. Consistent follow-up builds trust and demonstrates your commitment to your clients, showing that you truly care about their success. Remember, a strong sales pipeline requires constant nurturing, not just initial bursts of energy.

3.4 Client Onboarding

A smooth onboarding process is crucial; it sets the tone for the entire client relationship. Think of it as the foundation upon which you'll build trust and long-term success. A well-structured onboarding process not only clarifies expectations but also ensures both you and your client are on the same page from the start, minimizing misunderstandings and potential conflicts later. Efficiently onboarding new clients streamlines your workflow and contributes to increased productivity, allowing you to focus on delivering exceptional services.

First impressions matter immensely. Before the client's official start date, send a personalized welcome email. Include details like confirming the project scope, agreed-upon timeline, and initial communication points. This proactive approach demonstrates professionalism and sets a positive expectation for the working relationship. Consider adding a brief personal touch, perhaps mentioning something specific you discussed during the sales process, to reinforce your connection. This small gesture can create a welcoming atmosphere for the client.

The kickoff meeting is your chance to further solidify the relationship. Aim for a video call to allow for a more personal and engaging interaction. During this meeting, review the project scope once more, clarifying any remaining questions or ambiguities. Discuss the client's expectations in detail, actively listening to their concerns and addressing them promptly. This collaborative approach builds trust and demonstrates your commitment to understanding their needs. Remember to clearly outline your process and any relevant tools you'll be using, ensuring transparency from day one.

Establish clear communication channels and protocols early on. Will you primarily communicate via email, instant messaging, or project management software? Set expectations for response times, ensuring realistic deadlines for your communication and your client's, avoiding frustrating delays. Consider using a project management tool; it helps to centralize communication, track progress, and manage deadlines effectively. Shared documents, progress updates, and feedback all become organized within the platform. A consistent communication strategy minimizes confusion and ensures efficiency.

Throughout the project, consistent check-ins are vital. Regular updates, preferably scheduled in advance, maintain open communication. These check-ins offer opportunities for feedback, addressing any emerging challenges, and keeping the project on track. By proactively identifying potential problems and solving them early, you avoid major setbacks and preserve the client's confidence. Schedule short, frequent check-ins rather than infrequent, long ones; this approach fosters more effective collaboration and allows for quick resolution of issues.

Finally, gather client feedback at the conclusion of the project. This is not just about asking if they're satisfied, but gathering constructive criticism to enhance your services. A simple survey or even a brief call can provide valuable insights. Use this feedback not only for improving future projects but also to demonstrate your commitment to continuous improvement. Sharing the improvements you've made based on their feedback further strengthens client relationships and demonstrates your value as a service provider. Client satisfaction should always be a primary goal, ensuring they feel heard and valued.

3.5 Pricing Your Services

Setting your prices correctly is crucial; it directly impacts your profitability and your business's perception. Underpricing can lead to financial struggles, while overpricing can deter potential clients. Finding the sweet spot requires careful consideration of several factors. It isn't about arbitrarily choosing a number; it's about a strategic approach. It's about valuing your skills and experience while remaining competitive in your market.

Your time is valuable. Calculate your hourly rate by considering your expenses, desired income, and the time spent on each service. Remember to include not only direct work hours but also time spent on administrative tasks, marketing, and client communication. This comprehensive approach ensures accurate pricing that reflects your total investment. This isn't just about earning money; it's about recognizing the true worth of your efforts. Don't undervalue yourself.

Competitor analysis is key. Research what similar businesses in your area or online charge for comparable services. This doesn't necessarily mean copying their prices, but it helps you understand the market range and adjust accordingly. Consider their pricing strategies and target markets, noting any niches where you can offer unique value. Understand their position and consider how your services may stand out.

Value-based pricing focuses on the benefits your services provide, not just the cost of your time. What problems do you solve for your clients? How do your services improve their lives or businesses? Quantify these benefits and reflect them in your pricing. High-value services often command higher prices due to the substantial positive impact they offer. This is what elevates you from being a service provider to a solution provider.

Packaging your services strategically is important for streamlining your offers and maximizing profits. Create packages that combine several services at a discounted price, encouraging clients to purchase more comprehensive solutions. Offering various package levels gives clients options that fit their budget and needs. You can create bundles that cater to different client segments. Offering additional services for an up-charge can also increase revenue streams.

Consider offering different payment options. Not all clients pay the same way or prefer the same thing. Allowing clients to pay through multiple channels like credit cards, payment platforms, or even installments can broaden your client base and increase sales. Be clear about your payment terms and conditions. Be adaptable; the ability to accommodate various payment choices reflects flexibility and understanding.

Transparency is vital in fostering trust. Clearly outline your pricing structure on your website and in your communications. Avoid hidden fees or unexpected costs. This builds client confidence. They know exactly what they're getting and what they will pay; this is key to creating lasting, positive client relations. Transparency leads to greater peace of mind.

Review and adjust your pricing regularly. Market conditions, your experience, and your service offerings may evolve over time. Periodically review your pricing to ensure it remains competitive and profitable. Regular review keeps your services aligned with your target market and financial goals. Regular checks are key for long-term growth and profitability. Don't be afraid to adapt and evolve your pricing strategy.

Finally, remember that pricing is just one piece of the puzzle. Excellent customer service, effective marketing, and a strong reputation are equally vital to success. Pricing, when perfectly balanced, becomes a strategic tool in a complete business plan. It's part of a larger strategy for building a sustainable and prosperous future. Your pricing is a reflection of your worth and your business's value proposition.

4 Customer Relationship Magic

Exceptional customer service isn't just about solving problems; it's about building relationships. It's about turning one-time clients into loyal advocates who actively recommend your services. This requires a proactive and personalized approach, far beyond simply responding to inquiries. Think of it as weaving a tapestry of positive interactions that strengthens over time, each thread representing a meaningful connection.

Building strong client relationships begins with clear and consistent communication. Respond promptly to emails and messages, ensuring your tone is professional yet friendly. Avoid overly formal language that might create a distance. Instead, aim for a conversational style that fosters rapport. Regularly update clients on project progress, even if there are no significant developments. A simple "checking in" email demonstrates that you value their business and are committed to delivering exceptional service. This consistent communication reinforces the feeling of being valued.

Proactive communication is equally crucial. Don't wait for clients to reach out with problems; anticipate their needs. For example, send them relevant articles or resources that might be helpful. Offer helpful advice or insights related to their industry or business goals. Such gestures show you're invested in their success, going above and beyond what's typically expected. These small acts of kindness can make a significant difference in building loyalty.

Personalized communication is key to fostering genuine connections. Remember client details like birthdays or work anniversaries. A simple greeting card or email acknowledging these occasions demonstrates that you pay attention and value their relationship. This personalized touch transforms a transactional relationship into a meaningful one. It creates an emotional connection that strengthens over time. This personalized touch makes a huge difference.

Beyond communication, exceeding client expectations is vital. Go the extra mile. If a client expresses a challenge, brainstorm solutions together. If you notice something that could improve their process or product, offer suggestions. This collaborative approach shows you are a partner in their success. It transforms the service relationship into a collaborative venture. Remember, they're not just buying your service; they are partnering with you.

Actively solicit feedback. Regularly ask your clients for their input on your services. This demonstrates that you value their opinions and are open to improvement. Use the feedback to refine your offerings and enhance the overall client experience. Moreover, it helps you gain insights into what clients truly value and where you might be able to improve. This continuous feedback loop is invaluable.

Implement a CRM system to keep track of all your client interactions. It is important to document not only sales information, but also any personal details that could help you maintain a more personalized approach. A CRM, when used correctly, allows you to keep track of each interaction, making for a seamless and efficient experience. Using technology in this way helps elevate customer service and relationship build-

ing.
Don't underestimate the power of a simple "thank you." Expressing sincere gratitude for their business is a powerful way to show appreciation. A handwritten note or a personalized email can leave a lasting impression. It's not only good manners, but it strengthens the bond you have created with your customer. Small acts of gratitude can have a significant impact. They strengthen the emotional connection.

Remember, customer relationship management is an ongoing process. It's a continuous journey of building trust and fostering loyalty. It requires consistent effort and dedication. However, the rewards—increased customer retention, positive word-of-mouth referrals, and a thriving business—are well worth the investment. Building strong client relationships forms the backbone of a sustainable business, transforming your work environment into a thriving community. The success you build is not only based on quality service, but on strong relationships built over time and careful tending.

4.1 Communication Excellence

Clear, concise communication is the cornerstone of successful client relationships. It's not just about exchanging information; it's about building trust, understanding, and ultimately, loyalty. Ambiguity breeds misunderstanding, lost opportunities, and potentially, damaged reputations. Mastering clear communication means proactively addressing potential issues before they escalate, fostering a positive and productive working relationship with every client. This proactive approach is paramount to the success of any solopreneur.

Active listening is more than simply hearing words; it's about truly understanding your client's needs and concerns. Paying close attention to both verbal and nonverbal cues – body language, tone of voice – allows you to grasp the complete message, not just the surface level. This demonstrates respect and shows your clients that you value their input. It fosters a deeper connection that transcends simple transactions, creating a solid foundation for long-term partnerships. Never underestimate the power of truly listening to what your clients are saying, both explicitly and implicitly.

Effective communication goes beyond just listening; it's about expressing your thoughts and ideas clearly and concisely. Avoid jargon or technical terms your clients might not understand. Instead, use plain language, ensuring your message is easily digestible. This prevents misinterpretations, keeps the conversation flowing smoothly, and most importantly, guarantees everyone is on the same page. Remember, your client's understanding is paramount – technical expertise is only beneficial if it can be effectively communicated.

Responsiveness is critical. Answering emails promptly, returning phone calls swiftly, and acknowledging inquiries efficiently all demonstrate professionalism and respect for your client's time. In today's fast-paced world, prompt communication often sets businesses apart. Being timely doesn't necessarily imply immediate responses for every inquiry, but aiming for a consistent and reasonable turnaround time allows you to set realistic expectations and maintain a positive client experience. Remember consistency breeds trust and reinforces your commitment.

Choose your communication channels strategically. For complex projects or sensitive matters, a phone call or video conference might be more effective than email, offering immediate clarification and fostering a personal connection. Conversely, email is suitable for routine updates or sharing documents. However, tailor your approach to each individual client and circumstance; one size does not fit all. Consider their preferred methods, their time constraints, and the nature of the information being conveyed.

Documentation is crucial. Keep detailed records of all communications – emails, phone calls, meeting notes – to avoid misunderstandings and ensure everyone remains informed. This is especially beneficial in resolving potential disagreements and ensuring consistency in your service delivery. Detailed records act as a valuable source of reference and protect you from potential disputes, providing tangible evidence of agreed-upon terms and completed actions. Make record-keeping a habit, a part of your standard operational procedure, to avoid future complications.

Proactive communication prevents potential problems. Instead of waiting for issues to arise, proactively update your clients on project progress, potential delays, or any relevant changes. This transparent approach builds trust and keeps clients informed, minimizing the chance of unexpected surprises and potential frustration. Regular updates demonstrate your accountability and commitment to the project's success, fostering a stronger relationship built on mutual understanding.

Beyond project updates, utilize different communication methods to nurture your relationships. A simple thank-you note after a successful project, a personalized email on their birthday, or a brief check-in phone call can go a long way in demonstrating that you value the relationship and aren't simply focused on transactions. This thoughtful approach establishes you as a trusted advisor, differentiating your services and enhancing long-term client retention. These seemingly small gestures contribute significantly to building strong, enduring relationships.

Conflict resolution is an inevitable aspect of business. When conflicts arise, address them promptly and directly. Listen to your client's perspective, express empathy, and work collaboratively towards a solution. This approach showcases your commitment to finding fair and equitable outcomes that preserve the relationship. Remember, conflict resolution isn't about winning an argument but about maintaining client trust and ensuring their satisfaction, even in challenging situations. Aim for mutually beneficial resolutions every time.

Finally, remember that communication is a two-way street. Encourage open dialogue and actively seek feedback from your clients. This shows your willingness to adapt and improve your services, fostering a stronger, more collaborative relationship. Client feedback is invaluable. It provides crucial insights into their experiences, allowing you to identify areas for improvement and enhance the overall quality of your services. Actively soliciting feedback demonstrates your commitment to excellence and client satisfaction. Use every opportunity to cultivate a relationship built on clear, honest, and respectful communication.

4.2 Building Loyalty

Client loyalty isn't merely about happy customers; it's the bedrock of a thriving solopreneur business. It's about fostering deep, lasting relationships that translate into repeat business, referrals, and ultimately, sustainable growth. Think of it not as a transaction, but as the beginning of a valuable partnership.

Building this loyalty requires a multifaceted approach, going beyond simply providing a good service or product. It necessitates genuine engagement, proactive communication, and a commitment to exceeding expectations. Consider how you can consistently surprise and delight your clients – perhaps with unexpected bonuses, personalized touches, or helpful resources that go above and beyond their initial purchase. Small gestures, thoughtfully implemented, can create significant impact.

Exceptional customer service is non-negotiable. This means being readily available, responding promptly to queries, and addressing concerns with empathy and efficiency. Imagine yourself in your client's shoes – what would make their experience seamless and enjoyable? Proactive problem-solving, before issues even arise, demonstrates foresight and strengthens the bond of trust. For example, sending a follow-up email after a project's completion asking for feedback, not just on your work, but also on how you can improve their experience, showcases a genuine interest in their needs.

Regular communication is key to maintaining a vibrant relationship. This doesn't mean bombarding clients with irrelevant emails; instead, it's about offering valuable content, sharing updates about your business, and maintaining a consistent, friendly presence. This could involve newsletters showcasing your expertise, social media interaction, or even personalized updates related to projects you've completed together. The goal is to stay top-of-mind, not just as a provider but also as a valuable resource and a trusted partner.

Gathering client feedback is paramount. Don't just passively wait for complaints; actively solicit input. Conduct regular surveys, ask for reviews, and make personal contact to check in on your clients. These interactions help gauge your performance and give invaluable insight into areas that could be improved. Remember, the feedback is crucial for growth; it's not about criticizing you but enhancing your understanding of your clientele. Use feedback to improve not only your products or services but also your customer interaction strategies, reinforcing the idea that you value their voice and opinion.

Implementing a loyalty program can significantly boost retention. This doesn't have to be complex; it could involve a simple points system, exclusive discounts for repeat customers, or early access to new products or services. The point is to reward loyalty and make clients feel appreciated for their continued support. Tailor your program to reflect your brand and the nature of your business; a generic points system might not work as well as a system that recognizes unique client contributions.

Finally, remember that building loyalty is an ongoing process, not a destination. It requires consistent effort, genuine care, and a commitment to long-term relationships. Think about your most loyal clients – what is it about your interactions with them that fosters such enduring connections? By continuously refining your approach based on feedback, adaptation, and a genuine concern for your clients, you'll create a loyal client base that becomes the engine of your business success. The key is to consistently build trust, showing clients that you value them beyond the immediate transaction. That's where the real magic happens. Nurture this carefully, and you'll harvest a reward far greater than fleeting sales: sustained success built upon a foundation of trust and reciprocal respect.

5 Time Management Mastery

Effective time management is the cornerstone of a thriving solopreneurship. Without it, even the most brilliant business ideas can crumble under the weight of unfocused efforts and missed deadlines. Mastering your time isn't about working more; it's about working smarter. It's about prioritizing tasks, streamlining workflows, and ultimately, creating more time for what truly matters – growing your business and enjoying a balanced life.

The Pareto Principle, or the 80/20 rule, is your secret weapon. Identify the 20% of your activities that generate 80% of your results. These are your high-impact tasks, the ones demanding immediate attention. Focus relentlessly on these, delegating or postponing less crucial tasks to avoid getting bogged down in minutiae. This deliberate focus allows you to maximize your output and achieve significant progress each day.

Prioritization isn't just about urgency; it's also about importance. A critical task might not be urgent today, but neglecting it can lead to significant problems down the line. Employ tools like Eisenhower Matrix, categorizing tasks by urgency and importance. This clear visual allows you to schedule high-impact tasks while strategically planning less urgent but crucial activities. This structured approach avoids firefighting and allows for proactive problem-solving, preventing the crisis management that often eats into productive time.

Batch similar tasks together. Instead of constantly switching between writing emails, making phone calls, and creating social media posts, dedicate specific time blocks to each activity. This minimizes context switching, a notorious productivity killer, leading to improved focus and efficiency. This reduces mental fatigue and allows for deeper engagement in each activity. You'll find you accomplish more in less time.

Embrace the power of technology. Project management tools like Trello, Asana, or Monday.com can help you organize tasks, set deadlines, and track progress effectively. These tools offer collaborative features, valuable even if you work solely, providing a system for organizing both personal and business tasks. Automated scheduling tools for email and social media can also free up significant time.

Delegation is a critical skill, even for solopreneurs. Outsource tasks that don't require your unique skills. This might involve hiring a virtual assistant for administrative work, or using freelance platforms for specific projects, such as graphic design or website development. Delegating frees up your time for tasks that directly contribute to your core business functions. Remember, you can't do everything yourself, and the smart entrepreneur knows when to seek assistance.

Time blocking is a simple, but incredibly powerful technique. Allocate specific time blocks for specific activities in your day. Schedule your most demanding tasks during periods of peak productivity, typically in the morning. This proactive time allocation ensures that your most important work gets done, and prevents less crucial tasks from consuming your entire day. Include buffer time to accommodate unexpected delays and avoid feeling overwhelmed.

Regularly review your schedule and refine your approach. What works for you today may not work tomorrow. Constantly evaluating your time management strategies, adapting to changing circumstances, and iterating on what proves effective is essential. This continuous self-reflection process guarantees continuous improvement and ensures your systems align with your goals. Regular reviews, perhaps weekly or monthly, are vital for identifying areas needing improvement and optimizing your time management systems further.

Avoid multitasking; it's a myth. While it might seem like you're accomplishing more by juggling multiple tasks simultaneously, the opposite is true. Your brain isn't built for multitasking; it switches rapidly between tasks, resulting in reduced efficiency and increased errors. Focus on one task at a time, fully immerse yourself in it, and then move on to the next.

Self-care isn't a luxury, it's a necessity. A well-rested, healthy you is a more productive you. Prioritize sleep, exercise, and mindful breaks throughout your day. These aren't time wasters; they're investments in your productivity and overall well-being. A burnout solopreneur is a non-productive solopreneur. Maintain a healthy work-life balance, and see the tangible benefits in your energy levels and focus.

Regularly review your progress and adjust your time management strategies accordingly. What works one week might not work the next. Continuous evaluation allows for refinement and optimization. Time management isn't a one-size-fits-all approach, it's a personal process of discovery and adaptation. Remember, consistent improvement is key to mastering your time. The journey to time management mastery is an ongoing one, requiring consistent effort and thoughtful reflection. The rewards, however, are well worth the investment.

5.1 Prioritization Techniques

Effective time management is the backbone of any successful solopreneur's operation. Without it, even the most brilliant ideas can crumble under the weight of unmanaged tasks and deadlines. Understanding prioritization is paramount, not just for completing your to-do list, but for achieving your overall business goals and maintaining a healthy work-life balance.

The Eisenhower Matrix, often called the Urgent-Important Matrix, provides a simple yet powerful framework. Categorize each task based on its urgency and importance. Urgent and important tasks demand immediate attention; these are your fires to extinguish. Important but not urgent tasks are your strategic planning and preventative maintenance – the things that prevent future fires. Urgent but not important tasks are often distractions, things others want you to do that don't significantly contribute to your business's success. Finally, tasks that are neither urgent nor important are best delegated or eliminated altogether. This method brings clarity and focus to your daily workload, preventing you from getting bogged down in less important tasks.

Learning to say "no" is a critical skill for any solopreneur. Constantly adding tasks, especially those that don't align with your long-term goals, only leads to overwhelm and burnout. Prioritize your time and energy; choose projects that genuinely contribute to your business objectives. Politely declining requests that don't fit your current capacity protects your time and allows you to focus on higher-priority initiatives. This isn't about being rude, but rather about strategically managing your resources – your most valuable resource being your time. Remember, a focused approach yields far greater results than spreading yourself too thin.

Motivate yourself using the Pareto Principle, often referred to as the 80/20 rule. It suggests that 80% of your results come from 20% of your efforts. Identifying that crucial 20% is key. Analyze your tasks. Which 20% consistently deliver the most significant impact on your business? Focus your energy on those high-impact activities first. This means strategically scheduling your most important tasks for when you're most alert and productive. Don't underestimate the power of understanding your personal peak performance times.

Another powerful technique is the "Eat the Frog" method. Identify your most challenging or unpleasant task – your "frog" – and tackle it first thing in the morning. Getting it out of the way early removes a significant weight from your shoulders, allowing you to approach the rest of your day with increased energy and confidence. This method is surprisingly effective at breaking through inertia and making significant progress early on. It's a powerful mental trick that can boost productivity considerably.

Regularly review and reassess your priorities. What worked last week might not be as effective this week. Your priorities should be dynamic, adapting to changing circumstances and business demands. Schedule time for weekly or monthly reviews to analyze your progress, identify roadblocks, and adjust your priorities as needed. This iterative approach ensures that you remain focused on the most impactful tasks, maximizing your productivity and achieving your goals efficiently. This is not a one-time process; it's a continuous cycle of refinement and adaptation.

Prioritization isn't just about tackling tasks; it's about aligning your actions with your vision. Make sure your daily tasks contribute to your overarching business goals. If a task doesn't align with your bigger picture, consider its value and whether it's worth your time and energy. This holistic approach ensures that you're not just busy, but that you're actively working towards sustainable success. By connecting your daily activities to your long-term objectives, you maintain a sense of purpose and direction.

The key to effective prioritization isn't about finding a magic bullet; it's about developing a personalized system that works for you. Experiment with different techniques. See what resonates with your personality and your work style. Develop a system that suits your preferences and enhances your productivity. Remember that finding the right combination might take some experimentation but the payoff in time management is worth the effort. The ultimate goal is to build a sustainable workflow that helps you achieve success without burnout.

5.2 Productivity Hacks

Harnessing the power of "deep work" is crucial. This involves scheduling dedicated blocks of uninterrupted time for your most demanding tasks. Eliminate distractions – silence your phone, close unnecessary browser tabs, and let your colleagues know you need focused time. Experiment with different time blocks, perhaps starting with 90-minute intervals, to find what suits your rhythm best. The key is consistency; make this a regular part of your routine. Remember to incorporate breaks to avoid burnout, and you'll find your concentration and output significantly improved.

Prioritize ruthlessly. Every solopreneur faces a mountain of tasks. The Pomodoro Technique can be invaluable; work in focused bursts of 25 minutes, followed by a short break. This structured approach can help you tackle projects systematically without feeling overwhelmed. Learn to distinguish between urgent and important tasks; focus on what truly moves the needle in your business, not just what screams loudest for attention. Using a task management system, whether digital or analog, can help tremendously with this prioritization process.

Batch similar tasks. Instead of constantly switching between different activities, group similar tasks together. For example, respond to all emails at once, make all your phone calls in a single block, or tackle all your social media updates during a designated period. This reduces mental switching costs, allowing you to enter a flow state and complete tasks more efficiently. This mindful approach can prevent you from feeling scattered and maximize your effectiveness.

Embrace technology wisely. Numerous apps and tools are designed to boost productivity. Explore options that streamline repetitive tasks, such as scheduling software, project management tools, or automation software for social media. However, avoid the trap of collecting too many tools; focus on a few high-impact solutions that genuinely enhance your workflow, avoiding the added complication of learning and managing multiple platforms.

Delegate effectively. Even as a solopreneur, outsourcing is not a sign of weakness but a strategic move. Identify time-consuming tasks that don't require your specific expertise and consider outsourcing them. This might involve hiring a virtual assistant for administrative tasks, engaging a freelance writer for content creation, or using a graphic design service for visuals. Careful selection of tasks to delegate will free up valuable time for high-value activities that only you can perform.

Regularly review your productivity strategies. What works today might not work tomorrow. Set aside time each week or month to reflect on your productivity levels. Analyze what's working well and identify areas for improvement. Experiment with different techniques, and don't be afraid to adjust your approach based on your experience. This continuous improvement cycle is vital for maximizing your efficiency as a solopreneur. A flexible approach is key to adapting and thriving.

Optimize your workspace. Your environment profoundly impacts productivity. Ensure your workspace is organized, comfortable, and free of distractions. This includes investing in ergonomic equipment to prevent physical discomfort and creating a space that inspires focus and creativity. Small adjustments, such as natural light or ambient sounds, can greatly improve your overall work experience.

Mindfulness and self-care. It might seem counterintuitive, but taking time for yourself is essential for sustained productivity. Practice mindfulness techniques, engage in regular exercise, and prioritize sufficient sleep. Burnout is a real threat for solopreneurs; self-care prevents it. By prioritizing your well-being, you improve your focus, creativity, and overall efficiency, ensuring a healthier and more productive workflow.

Learn to say "no." A common mistake for solopreneurs is overcommitment. Don't take on more than you can realistically handle. Learn to politely decline requests that don't align with your priorities or capacity. Protecting your time and energy is crucial for maintaining sustainable productivity. This crucial aspect of self-management will greatly impact your overall work efficiency.

Embrace the power of breaks. Short, regular breaks are critical for maintaining focus and preventing burnout. Step away from your workspace, stretch, take a walk, or simply close your eyes and breathe deeply. These short periods of rest will actually boost your overall productivity in the long run, by keeping your mind fresh and preventing mental fatigue. Incorporating these micro-breaks is far more effective than infrequent, longer breaks that disrupt your work flow.

5.3 Delegation Strategies

Many solopreneurs, myself included, initially resist delegation. The ingrained belief is that you must control every aspect to ensure quality. This, however, is a myth hindering growth. Effective delegation isn't about relinquishing control; it's about strategically assigning tasks to free up your time for high-impact activities that only you can do. Think of it as an investment in your business's future, not a sign of weakness.

Delegation isn't just for scaling; it's beneficial even when you're just starting. Perhaps you're spending too much time on administrative tasks, leaving little time for core business functions. Outsourcing data entry, social media scheduling, or even basic customer service inquiries can free up valuable hours. These hours could be spent on developing new products, refining your marketing strategy, or actively seeking new clients—all considerably more profitable uses of your time.

Start small. Don't jump into outsourcing complex projects immediately. Begin by identifying tasks that are repetitive, time-consuming, and don't require specialized knowledge. These are prime candidates for delegation. Once you've successfully delegated a few smaller tasks, you'll gain confidence and develop a system for assigning more complex projects later on. You'll also learn to better assess which tasks are worth outsourcing. This gradual approach helps avoid overwhelm and builds a solid foundation for future delegation.

Finding reliable help is crucial. Consider using freelancing platforms to source qualified individuals for specific tasks. Carefully review profiles, check references, and test their skills before committing to a larger project. Clear communication is paramount. Provide detailed instructions, set realistic deadlines, and maintain regular contact to ensure the work meets your standards. Think of the entire process as a collaborative project, not just a simple handover of duties. This collaborative approach fosters a sense of shared responsibility and can positively impact productivity.

Before you delegate, thoroughly document your processes. Create clear instructions, including step-by-step guides, templates, and examples. This ensures consistency and reduces the need for constant oversight. A well-defined process also allows you to scale more efficiently in the future, enabling you to easily onboard new team members or delegate more tasks without significant additional instruction. Imagine the efficiency: your systems working even while you're not directly involved.

Defining clear expectations is non-negotiable. Before delegating, explicitly communicate your expectations regarding quality, deadlines, and communication. Use a project management tool to track progress, provide feedback, and ensure everyone is on the same page. Regular check-ins, even for simple tasks, maintain transparency and allow for early course correction. This proactive approach minimizes potential issues and contributes to smoother workflow.

Successful delegation requires trust. Give your chosen assistant the autonomy to complete the task, providing support only when necessary. Micromanaging can stifle creativity and diminish efficiency. Instead, focus on the results, not the process. This fosters a positive working relationship and allows your team member to utilize their own strengths and initiative. Empowering individuals is empowering your business.

Remember to factor in the costs of delegation. While it can be extremely cost-effective, outsourcing does have associated expenses. Weigh the cost of outsourcing against the value of your time saved and the potential increase in revenue. This is a critical aspect of evaluating the overall Return on Investment (ROI) for any task delegated. It is not about simply saving money on labor; it's about generating more revenue in the long run.

Finally, regularly review your delegation strategy. What's working well? What needs improvement? Are there additional tasks you can delegate to further free up your time? Continuous evaluation is crucial for refinement and ensures that your delegation strategies remain effective and aligned with your evolving business needs. Adaptability is key to long-term success. By being open to adjustments and improvements, you optimize your efficiency and build a more resilient and profitable solopreneurship.

6 Legal & Business Structure

Choosing the right legal structure for your solopreneur venture is paramount. It's more than just a box to tick; it significantly impacts your liability, taxes, and even your future growth potential. A sole proprietorship, the simplest form, blends your personal and business liabilities. This means your personal assets are at risk if your business incurs debt or faces legal issues. Conversely, forming an LLC (Limited Liability Company) creates a separate legal entity, shielding your personal assets from business debts and lawsuits. The added layer of protection often outweighs the slightly increased administrative burden. Remember, consulting with a legal professional to determine the best fit for your specific circumstances is always recommended.

Beyond the basic structure, consider your long-term goals. Will you need to raise capital? An S-corp or a C-corp might be more suitable if you anticipate substantial growth and outside investment. These structures offer different tax advantages and shareholder responsibilities, but they come with a higher degree of administrative complexity. Don't rush into a decision based solely on perceived simplicity. Research thoroughly and weigh the advantages and disadvantages of each option carefully, considering both your current situation and your projected future. Your choice will directly influence your tax obligations, so thorough planning is essential.

Contracts are the backbone of your business dealings. A well-drafted contract protects you and your clients by clearly outlining expectations, payment terms, and responsibilities. Never underestimate the importance of having legally sound contracts in place for every significant transaction, whether it's a service agreement with a client, a lease for your workspace, or a partnership agreement with a collaborator. A poorly written or missing contract can lead to costly disputes and unresolved conflicts. Investing in legal expertise to review and draft contracts is a worthwhile investment that safeguards your business against potential risks.

Start with the basics. Learn about key contract components like offer and acceptance, consideration (the exchange of value), and legality. Ensure every contract clearly defines the scope of work, payment schedules, deadlines, and intellectual property rights. Include clauses detailing dispute resolution mechanisms and termination procedures, which act as a safety net against unforeseen circumstances. Remember, a contract is not just a formality; it is a vital document that protects your business interests and defines the parameters of your professional relationships.

Beyond client contracts, consider other essential agreements. A non-disclosure agreement (NDA) protects your confidential information, while an independent contractor agreement clarifies the relationship with freelancers or subcontractors. Understanding the nuances of different contract types and adapting them to your specific needs is crucial. While using pre-made templates might seem convenient, remember that a generic contract might not adequately address the unique aspects of your business. Therefore, seeking legal counsel is highly recommended, especially when dealing with significant contracts or complex business arrangements. The cost of avoiding a legal battle far outweighs the expense of professional legal advice.

Even with careful planning and robust contracts, unforeseen challenges can arise. Having a clear understanding of relevant laws and regulations related to your industry is vital. Familiarize yourself with consumer protection laws, tax regulations, and intellectual property rights. Staying abreast of these legal aspects is an ongoing process, so consider engaging a legal professional for ongoing guidance and advice. Remember, proactive legal management is not just about mitigating risk; it's also about ensuring your business operates efficiently and ethically. It contributes to building a trustworthy reputation with clients and partners, strengthening your position in the market.

6.1 Choosing a Structure

Choosing the right legal structure for your solopreneur venture is a crucial step, often overlooked in the initial excitement. It impacts everything from your tax obligations and liability protection to your ability to raise capital and even your credibility with potential clients. Don't underestimate the significance of this decision; it's a foundational element that will shape your business journey.

A sole proprietorship is the simplest form, blending your personal and business identities. This means you directly receive all profits but also bear full personal liability for any business debts or lawsuits. It's easy to set up, requiring minimal paperwork and administrative burden. However, the lack of separation between your personal and business assets can expose your personal finances to significant risk.

A limited liability company (LLC) offers a more protective structure.

Think of it as a shield separating your personal assets from business liabilities. While still relatively straightforward to establish, it provides a critical layer of protection against lawsuits or business debts, safeguarding your personal possessions. The increased complexity compared to a sole proprietorship is often worth the added security. Furthermore, LLCs can offer flexible tax options, allowing you to choose between being taxed as a sole proprietorship or a corporation, depending on your specific financial needs and goals.

Choosing between an LLC and a sole proprietorship hinges on your risk tolerance and the nature of your business. If your work involves higher risk – say, consulting for high-profile clients or operating in a field with potential legal exposure – the added protection of an LLC is highly recommended. For simpler businesses with minimal risk, the straightforwardness of a sole proprietorship might suffice, although the personal liability factor remains paramount.

For businesses anticipating significant growth or external investment, a corporation, either S-corp or C-corp, might be more suitable. These structures offer the strongest legal protection and potentially better opportunities for raising capital through equity financing. However, they come with increased administrative complexities, including more stringent record-keeping requirements, and potentially higher ongoing costs related to compliance and taxation. The decision to incorporate requires careful consideration and possibly professional legal and financial advice. Do not underestimate the importance of consulting an expert to carefully weigh the pros and cons for your specific circumstances.

The complexity doesn't end with the structure itself; you must also consider your state's specific regulations and requirements. Each state has its unique rules regarding registration, filing fees, and ongoing compliance for various business entities. It's critical to thoroughly research your state's requirements before making a decision, or else risk facing penalties. Seek professional advice to navigate this, as the specifics can be intricate and vary dramatically between jurisdictions.

Remember, the best structure is one that aligns with your business's current needs and future aspirations. A structure that is perfectly suited for a startup might become inefficient as the business expands, requiring a change down the road. Regularly review your structure's suitability to your evolving needs. Consider consulting with a legal professional or business advisor to ensure your chosen structure is optimal, and to understand any potential limitations or tax implications associated with your selection. They can guide you through the complexities of state regulations, helping you make an informed decision that safeguards your interests and paves the way for successful growth. This proactive approach will pay dividends in the long run, helping you avoid costly mistakes and ensuring the sustainability of your venture.

Your choice of structure isn't just a legal formality; it's a strategic decision that will directly influence your business's financial health, liability protection, and future growth. Don't rush into this critical decision; take your time, thoroughly research the options, and seek professional counsel if needed. The structure you choose today will underpin the success and security of your solopreneur journey for years to come. Proactive planning in this area will contribute significantly to the overall success and longevity of your business. So, before you launch into operations, get the structure right. It sets the stage for everything that follows. This initial step provides a solid foundation, ensuring your future self will thank you for the time invested in choosing wisely. Ignoring this crucial foundation could have significant repercussions, impacting your business's security and your personal financial well-being.

6.2 Contracts & Agreements

Contracts are the backbone of any successful business, especially for solopreneurs. They protect your interests, clarify expectations, and prevent misunderstandings. Without them, you're operating on shaky ground, vulnerable to disputes and potential financial losses. Think of a contract as a safety net, a clear outline of the rules of engagement between you and your clients, ensuring everyone is on the same page. This reduces the risk of conflict and makes the whole business more efficient. Crafting a well-written contract requires more than just a generic template downloaded from the internet. It necessitates understanding the specific needs of your business and your client's project. A generic contract might not cover all the potential issues related to your unique field. This is true even if you're just starting out; taking the time to properly structure the contract based on what your business does is a crucial element of success. Consider consulting with a legal professional to tailor it to your specific circumstances, especially in the beginning when your experience is limited.

Remember that a contract is not simply a legal document; it's a statement of your professionalism and commitment to your clients. A well-structured and thoughtfully worded contract shows you are serious about your business and are dedicated to delivering what is agreed upon. It's a sign of respect for your client's investment of time and resources. Clients will likely perceive you as more professional and reliable if you have them sign a well-drafted contract, strengthening their confidence in your capabilities. This builds trust and loyalty, crucial elements for long-term client relationships.

Negotiation is a key aspect of the contract process. You need to understand the requirements of your client and what their needs are. It's not about winning or losing, but about finding common ground that is mutually acceptable, where the agreement accurately reflects both your needs and your client's needs. It requires clear and open communication, listening actively to your client's concerns and addressing any reservations they may have. Remember to be assertive yet accommodating, maintaining a professional and collaborative approach throughout the discussion.

Beyond the initial contract, think about potential future collaborations. This could involve a clear outline for how your future projects will be handled, and it shows foresight. Establish a process for handling amendments or changes to the contract. Having a streamlined approach ensures efficiency and avoids disputes over added services or modifications to the original plan. This protects both you and your client. This proactive approach shows your clients you are organized and that you anticipate potential challenges, further solidifying your reputation as a professional and dependable service provider. Consider including clauses addressing potential issues that might arise in the course of a long-term project, so it addresses everything from the start.

Intellectual property rights are particularly important for solopreneurs, especially if your work involves creative elements or specialized knowledge. Your contracts must clearly define ownership and usage rights. Ensure that you retain the rights to your work unless otherwise explicitly agreed upon in writing. This prevents potential future conflicts and ensures you are legally protected from unauthorized use of your intellectual property. If you are unclear about intellectual property, it's essential to seek professional legal guidance to ensure your contracts are compliant with relevant laws and regulations. This proactive approach will protect your future and the value of your creations.

Consider including a payment schedule, payment terms, and a clear description of the deliverables in your contracts. It defines precisely what you will deliver, when you will deliver it, and how much compensation you will receive. This clarity prevents misunderstandings and payment disputes down the line. Consider using clear, concise language, avoiding jargon or technical terms that may not be understood by your clients. It is advisable to avoid making your contract unnecessarily long and overly complicated. This is crucial not only for managing your finances but also for maintaining positive relationships with your clients.

Always keep a copy of every contract for your records. Maintain a secure system for storing these documents. This system will allow you to easily access them if needed. Having these readily accessible allows you to reference the details quickly if disputes arise. This diligent approach to record-keeping is invaluable in protecting your business and ensuring your continued success. Good record-keeping is part of showing your clients that you are a professional, reliable, and detailed service provider.

Finally, remember that even the best contracts cannot anticipate every eventuality. Be prepared to handle unforeseen circumstances gracefully and professionally. Sometimes, flexibility and compromise are necessary to maintain strong client relationships. However, this should always be within the framework of the original contract. A willingness to work collaboratively and resolve issues amicably showcases your professionalism and strengthens your reputation. It's a critical component of maintaining long-term client relationships and building a successful solopreneur business. Remember, a contract is a tool to support a mutually beneficial and sustainable relationship.

7 Growth & Sustainability

Scaling your solo business requires a strategic approach, moving beyond simply handling day-to-day tasks. It's about creating a system that allows for growth without compromising the quality that defines your brand. Imagine a well-oiled machine, each part contributing to a smooth, efficient whole—that's the goal. You'll need to identify your business's core strengths, the areas where you excel and generate the most value. Then, focus your energy there, delegating or outsourcing tasks that fall outside your expertise. Remember, focusing your efforts strategically is often more productive than trying to do everything yourself.

Long-term planning is paramount; it's not just about setting annual goals, but about charting a course for your business's future, five or even ten years down the line. Consider your ideal client, your target market, and the trajectory you envision. Visualize your business in its future state. What services will you offer? What market share do you hope to achieve? What kind of impact do you want to make? These are the questions to guide your long-term strategy. Having a well-defined path makes adapting to unexpected challenges easier.

Adapting to change is not merely reacting to external forces; it's about proactively anticipating market shifts and adjusting your strategies accordingly. Staying informed about industry trends, technological advancements, and changes in consumer behavior is crucial. This requires continuous learning and a willingness to experiment. Embrace flexibility; your business model shouldn't be rigid but adaptable to the ever-changing business landscape. Consider the possibility of pivoting—shifting your focus or offerings—if necessary. The key is to remain nimble, responsive, and open to new opportunities.

Financial forecasting extends beyond simply tracking income and expenses. It's about predicting future financial performance, based on your sales projections, market analysis, and operational costs. Create realistic financial models, incorporating variables that can impact your bottom line. This allows you to make informed decisions about investments, pricing, and resource allocation. Accurate forecasting enables you to secure funding if needed and makes it possible to plan for expansion or handle potential downturns. Avoid overly optimistic projections; realistic forecasting is crucial for long-term stability.

Building a team, if and when you're ready, should be a well-considered decision, not a knee-jerk reaction to increased workload. It's about finding individuals who complement your skills and share your vision. Begin by identifying the areas where you need support. Then, define the roles and responsibilities clearly. Establish a strong company culture, so your team members feel valued and motivated. Effective teamwork elevates the entire operation; it's not just about assigning tasks but fostering collaboration and shared success. Remember to invest in training and development to ensure your team's continuous growth. The quality of your team directly impacts your business's overall performance and sustainability. Thorough planning and recruitment are critical to building a strong, effective team. Consider outsourcing to a more established firm if there is already an established firm that has what you need.

7.1 Scaling Your Business

Scaling your business feels like climbing a mountain; the view from the top is breathtaking, but the ascent requires careful planning and consistent effort. Initially, you might feel like you're carrying the entire mountain on your back, juggling all aspects of the operation single-handedly. The key is to systematize your processes, allowing you to leverage your existing work without constantly reinventing the wheel. This isn't about hiring immediately; it's about optimizing your current workflow.

Start by identifying your most profitable services or products. What generates the most revenue with the least effort? Focus your energy there. Analyze your sales data meticulously; this isn't just about looking at numbers. It's about understanding why certain products or services are selling better than others. This understanding will inform your future strategies, ensuring that you prioritize efforts on high-yield activities. You'll also want to examine client feedback and testimonials to understand what resonates most effectively with your target audience. This information, coupled with your sales data, will provide a strong foundation for scaling strategically.

Consider outsourcing tasks that don't directly contribute to your core competencies. This isn't about replacing yourself; it's about freeing up your time to concentrate on higher-level activities such as strategic planning and business development. You could outsource tasks like customer service email responses, social media management, or even basic bookkeeping. The cost of outsourcing these responsibilities is often far outweighed by the increased efficiency and time saved, allowing you to focus on income-generating activities. Remember, even small, incremental improvements can greatly impact your bottom line.

As your business grows, developing strong relationships with other professionals becomes crucial. Build your network by attending industry events, joining online forums, and actively engaging with fellow entrepreneurs. Networking doesn't just mean collecting business cards; it's about fostering genuine connections and building mutually beneficial partnerships. These partnerships can provide invaluable support, collaboration opportunities, and even referrals, leading to substantial growth. Collaborations can be especially valuable; by sharing resources and expertise, you can expand your reach and tap into new markets. Look for individuals whose strengths complement your own.

Investing in efficient technology is essential for scaling. This might include Customer Relationship Management (CRM) software to streamline communication and track customer interactions. Think about project management tools to maintain clarity and organization across multiple projects. The right tools can significantly enhance productivity and free up valuable time that can be reinvested in growth initiatives. Implementing such systems might seem like an upfront cost, but in the long run, the increased efficiency and organization outweigh the initial investment, leading to significant returns. These tools facilitate efficient scaling because they allow you to manage a larger workload with the same (or even fewer) resources.

Don't neglect the importance of adapting to change. The business landscape is constantly evolving, and your ability to adapt and innovate is vital for long-term success. Regularly reassess your business strategies and be open to adjusting your plans as needed. Monitor market trends and competitors' actions, remaining flexible and responsive to changes in customer demand. A static business plan is a recipe for stagnation. Continuous improvement and adaptation are key elements in scaling effectively and sustainably. Remember to celebrate your successes along

the way; these milestones will motivate you to keep moving forward, especially during challenging times.
Finally, planning for the future is paramount. Create a long-term business plan that outlines your goals, strategies, and projections for the coming years. This plan should include financial forecasts, market analysis, and a roadmap for achieving your scaling objectives. Regularly review and update this plan to incorporate new insights, adapt to changing market conditions, and adjust your trajectory as needed. A well-defined plan provides a solid foundation for sustainable growth, helping you steer your business towards lasting success. It's not simply a document; it's a living guide that helps you stay focused and adapt as your business evolves. Remember, scaling is a marathon, not a sprint. Consistent effort, strategic planning, and adaptability are the cornerstones of sustainable growth.

7.2 Long-Term Planning

Long-term planning isn't about predicting the future; it's about creating a roadmap that adapts to its changes. Think of it as charting a course across an ocean – you know your general destination, but you'll need to adjust your sails based on the winds and currents you encounter. Successful solopreneurs don't just react to what happens; they anticipate potential obstacles and opportunities, positioning themselves for sustained success. This proactive approach minimizes risks and maximizes the potential for long-term profitability and personal satisfaction.
Your initial business plan is a crucial first step, but it shouldn't be a static document. Instead, view it as a living organism, constantly evolving and adapting to the changing landscape of your industry and your own personal growth. Regularly review and update your plan, perhaps quar-

terly or even monthly, incorporating lessons learned and adjusting your strategies accordingly. This continuous refinement is key to staying relevant and competitive.

Financial forecasting isn't just about crunching numbers; it's about understanding the story your numbers tell. Create realistic projections for your income, expenses, and profit margins. Consider different scenarios – best-case, worst-case, and most likely – to prepare for various possibilities. This preparation will help you make informed decisions about investments, pricing, and resource allocation, ensuring you're always a step ahead of the game. Remember, detailed forecasts aren't just about financial health; they're a crucial tool for securing funding, if needed, and demonstrating your business's viability to potential partners or investors.

Marketing is a marathon, not a sprint. Instead of focusing solely on short-term gains, build a long-term marketing strategy that fosters brand loyalty and consistent growth. This means creating a strong brand identity that resonates with your target audience, and employing marketing tactics—both online and offline—that are consistent and sustainable over the long term. Think about building relationships with influencers, participating in industry events, or even creating a loyal customer rewards program. These approaches contribute to a brand image that people remember and trust.

Customer relationships are the bedrock of any successful business, particularly for solopreneurs. Treat each client as an individual and nurture those relationships. Regular communication, personalized service, and proactive problem-solving build trust and loyalty—essential for long-term success. Consider offering exclusive content, early access to new products or services, or personalized discounts to your loyal customers.

This dedication creates a stronger emotional connection that fosters repeat business and referrals.

Scaling your business requires careful consideration of your capacity and resources. Don't rush into expansion without a well-defined plan. Identify your bottlenecks, whether it's time, technology, or team capacity. Strategically address these constraints to avoid overwhelming yourself and compromising the quality of your services. Remember, scaling successfully isn't about rapid growth at any cost; it's about sustainable growth that preserves your business's quality and profitability. Careful planning is critical to avoid common scaling pitfalls.

Finally, remember that adaptation is essential for long-term survival. The business landscape is constantly changing, and your business needs to evolve with it. Stay informed about industry trends, emerging technologies, and changes in consumer behavior. Be willing to pivot your strategies as needed and embrace change as an opportunity for growth rather than a threat. The most successful businesses are those that are agile and adaptable, constantly refining their approach to stay ahead of the curve. Continuous learning and adapting is vital for long-term success in the dynamic world of solopreneurship.

7.3 Adapting to Change

The solopreneur journey isn't a straight line; expect detours. Navigating the unpredictable requires adaptability, a skill honed through proactive planning and a willingness to embrace the unexpected. Think of your business plan as a flexible roadmap, not a rigid set of instructions.

Market trends shift, client needs evolve, and even your own passions might take you in new directions. Sticking to a plan that doesn't account for these changes is a recipe for stagnation, perhaps even failure. Instead, cultivate a mindset of continuous learning and refinement.

Regularly reassess your target market. Are their needs changing? Are competitors innovating? Perhaps a new technology has emerged, creating fresh opportunities or challenging your existing services. Stay informed through industry publications, networking events, and competitor analysis. This proactive monitoring allows you to anticipate shifts and adapt before they significantly impact your business.

Adapting isn't just about reacting to external forces; it also involves internal adjustments. Your business might start differently from how it ends up. Maybe your initial product resonates less than expected, and you need to pivot. This requires honesty, self-reflection, and the courage to change course. Don't be afraid to admit if your initial strategy isn't working and reallocate resources where they'll have the most impact.

Financial flexibility is crucial for navigating change. Maintaining a healthy financial cushion allows you to weather unexpected downturns or invest in new opportunities as they emerge. This emphasizes the importance of the earlier chapters on budgeting and expense tracking; strong financial foundations provide the stability needed to adapt effectively to shifting circumstances.

Think of your marketing strategy as a living document. What worked six months ago might not resonate now. A/B test your marketing efforts, continually refining your approach to optimize engagement and conversion rates. Monitor your website analytics, paying attention to traffic sources and user behavior. This data provides invaluable insights into what's working and what needs adjustment.

Similarly, client communication is key. Establish open channels for feedback; encourage customers to share their opinions, suggestions, and complaints. Use this feedback to improve your services, address issues promptly, and adapt to evolving client expectations. Remember, even negative feedback can be a valuable opportunity for improvement and growth.

The ability to adapt extends beyond your core business operations. Consider your personal well-being. Running a solo business can be intensely demanding. Building resilience involves setting boundaries, prioritizing self-care, and developing strategies to manage stress. This includes seeking support from mentors, peers, or even a therapist. Your well-being directly affects your adaptability and ultimately, your success.

Remember, adapting to change is not a one-time event, but an ongoing process. Embrace the uncertainty, celebrate small victories, learn from setbacks, and remain committed to learning and growth. By embracing change as an opportunity rather than a threat, you will greatly improve your chances of solopreneur success and longevity in the ever-evolving business landscape. Ultimately, adaptability is the key to long-term survival and prosperity.

7.4 Financial Forecasting

Accurate financial forecasting is crucial for the long-term health of your solopreneur venture. It's not just about predicting the future; it's about using data-driven insights to make informed decisions today, ensuring your business remains resilient and profitable. Without a clear understanding of your potential income and expenses, you risk making choices that hinder your progress. This chapter will arm you with the knowledge and techniques to build a dependable forecasting model.

Begin by gathering your historical data. This includes income statements, expense reports, and sales figures from the past year, or even longer if available. Analyze these records meticulously, identifying trends, seasonality, and any unexpected fluctuations. Did your sales spike during a particular holiday season? Did expenses increase during a specific project? Understanding these patterns is vital for creating accurate projections.

Next, consider external factors that might influence your business. This isn't merely speculation; it's informed research. Look at industry trends, economic forecasts, and potential changes in your target market. Will there be any significant price changes for your materials? Are new competitors entering the market? Are there upcoming economic events that might impact consumer spending? Incorporating these elements adds a layer of realism to your predictions.

Now, let's translate this data into actionable forecasts. There are several approaches, each with its own strengths. You might use a simple percentage-based projection, extrapolating past growth rates into the future. This is straightforward, but it may not account for market changes or unexpected developments. A more sophisticated method might involve employing a forecasting software or even consulting with a financial advisor. These tools can analyze your data more deeply and produce more detailed forecasts. Remember, the method you choose should depend on your business' complexity and your available resources.

For example, you could use a spreadsheet program to create a forecast. Input your historical data, and then make reasonable assumptions about future sales and expenses based on your research and understanding of market trends. Create separate columns for different revenue streams and expense categories, allowing for a granular analysis. This will give you a clearer picture of where your money is coming from and where it's going, a much more effective approach than relying on estimations alone. Remember to be conservative in your estimations. Overly optimistic forecasts can set unrealistic expectations.

Regularly review and adjust your forecasts. Your business is not static; it's constantly evolving. Market conditions change, new opportunities arise, and unexpected expenses occur. Therefore, it's not a "set it and forget it" process. Make it a habit to review your forecasts at least quarterly, comparing them to your actual performance. This allows you to identify discrepancies early on and make necessary adjustments to your business plan. This iterative approach enables you to maintain a flexible approach to your business strategy.

Don't be discouraged by unexpected deviations. Forecasts aren't crystal balls; they're tools for informed decision-making. When discrepancies arise between your forecasts and actual results, take time to analyze the reasons behind the differences. This will highlight areas that require further investigation, adjustments to your approach, and a review of your overall business strategy. These insights can be exceptionally valuable, guiding you towards more effective planning in the future. Financial forecasting is not simply a task; it is a learning opportunity.

Consider the possibility of creating multiple forecast scenarios. This allows you to plan for a range of possible outcomes, mitigating potential risks. This involves creating different scenarios based on a variety of possible market conditions. For example, you could create a best-case, worst-case, and most likely scenario. By anticipating various possibilities, you can prepare for unexpected occurrences and make better-informed decisions. Thinking ahead is critical for long-term resilience.

Finally, remember that financial forecasting is an integral part of your overall business planning. It isn't a separate entity; rather, it's intricately woven into your strategic decision-making. Use these forecasts not merely as predictions, but as instruments to guide your actions, shaping your marketing strategies, pricing decisions, and resource allocation. Financial forecasting is a journey, not a destination. Through continued vigilance and adaptation, you can create a business that stands the test of time. It's a critical skill for any solopreneur seeking long-term success. This process will transform the way you approach financial management and enhance your strategic insights.

7.5 Team Building (If Needed)

Many solopreneurs thrive independently, their businesses a testament to individual skill and dedication. However, growth often demands a shift; a point where expansion necessitates a team. This chapter addresses that transition, offering practical advice for solopreneurs considering building their first team.

Building a team isn't simply about hiring; it's a fundamental change in how you operate. It requires a significant investment, not only financially but also in time and energy. Before you even begin to think about job postings, you need to thoroughly assess your business needs. What specific roles are genuinely necessary for your business to grow? Can these tasks be outsourced initially, avoiding the immediate commitment of full-time employees? Carefully consider the implications – additional overhead costs, administrative burdens, and the added complexities of team management.

The initial steps involve carefully defining the roles and responsibilities within your growing organization. Create detailed job descriptions that clearly outline expectations, required skills, and reporting structures. This structured approach is essential for attracting qualified candidates and ensuring a smooth onboarding process. Avoid vague descriptions;

clarity is crucial for both you and potential hires. Be specific about required qualifications, experience, and even personality traits that would best fit your business culture, if you are building one.

Finding the right people is paramount. Rely on your network, utilize online job boards, and consider engaging recruitment agencies if your budget allows. Thoroughly vet candidates through multiple interview stages, paying attention not only to their technical skills but also their soft skills, their ability to work independently yet collaboratively, and their alignment with your business values. Check references and consider trial periods before making any permanent commitments. This careful selection process minimizes the risk of costly mis-hires.

Once you've assembled your team, invest time in establishing clear communication channels and processes. Regular meetings, whether weekly or bi-weekly, are essential for keeping everyone informed, addressing concerns, and ensuring alignment with business goals. Implement project management software to track progress, assign tasks, and maintain transparency. Establish a system for feedback—regular check-ins and performance reviews are crucial for maintaining motivation, addressing issues promptly, and fostering a positive work environment.

Beyond the practical aspects of hiring and management, consider the cultural impact of building a team. Your business culture will evolve, requiring adaptation on your part. This transition from solopreneur to team leader demands a shift in mindset; you'll need to delegate effectively, trust your team's abilities, and embrace collaborative decision-making. Building a strong team culture requires fostering trust, open communication, and mutual respect, creating an environment where everyone feels valued and empowered to contribute their best work.

Finally, remember that building a team is an ongoing process. It requires continuous investment in training, development, and fostering a strong team dynamic. Regularly assess your team's performance, identify areas for improvement, and adapt your management style as needed. This continuous adjustment is critical for ensuring your team's continued success and ensuring that your team aligns with the changing landscape of your business. Never underestimate the power of investing in your team's growth; a strong, well-supported team is the cornerstone of any successful and expanding business. The transition might be challenging, but with careful planning, diligent recruitment, and a commitment to fostering a positive work environment, you can successfully build a team that propels your business to new heights. Remember that building a team isn't a one-time event; it's a long-term commitment that requires ongoing nurturing and adaptation.

www.ingramcontent.com/pod-product-compliance
Lightning Source LLC
LaVergne TN
LVHW022023200926
848481LV00007B/2516